Dear Parents,

Children's earliest experiences with stories and books usually involve grown-ups reading to them. However, reading should be active, and as adults, we can help young readers make meaning of the text by prompting them to relate the book to what they already know and to their personal experiences. Our questions will lead them to move beyond the simple story and pictures and encourage them to think beneath the surface. For example, after reading a story about the sleep habits of animals, you might ask, "Do you remember when you moved into a big bed? Could you see the moon out of your window?"

Illustrations in these books are wonderful and can be used in a variety of ways. Your questions about them can direct the child to details and encourage him or her to think about what those details tell us about the story. You might ask the child to find three different "beds" used by animals and insects in the book. Illustrations can even be used to inspire readers to draw their own pictures related to the text.

At the end of each book, there are some suggested questions and activities related to the story. These questions range in difficulty and will help you move young readers from the text itself to thinking skills such as comparing and contrasting, predicting, applying what they learned to new situations and identifying things they want to find out more about. This conversation about their reading may even result in the children becoming the storytellers, rather than simply the listeners!

Harriet Ziefert, M.A.
Language Arts/Reading Specialist

More to **Think**  **About**

Does a Woodpecker Use a Hammer?

Does a Beaver Sleep in a Bed?

Does a Camel Cook Spaghetti?

Does a Panda Go to School?

Does an Owl Wear Eyeglasses?

Does a Tiger Go to the Dentist?

Doe a Hippo Go to the Doctor?

Does a Seal Smile?

Think **About** what everyone wears

Does a Bear Wear Boots?

Harriet Ziefert • illustrations by **Emily Bolam**

BLUE APPLE

Text copyright © 2005, 2014 by Harriet Ziefert
Illustrations copyright © 2005 by Emily Bolam
All rights reserved
CIP data is available.
Published in the United States 2014 by
🍎 Blue Apple Books
515 Valley Street, Maplewood, NJ 07040
www.blueapplebooks.com
Printed in China
ISBN: 978-1-60905-424-3
1 3 5 7 9 10 8 6 4 2
02/14

Who wears clothes?
Does a chimp?

Chimps do not wear clothes.
They wear clothes only
when dressed by people.

Does a donkey wear clothes?

A donkey might wear a straw hat
while working in the hot sun.

But you will never see a donkey
with a shirt and trousers!

Does a polar bear wear boots?

Never!
A polar bear has hairy pads on its feet
and thick fur on its legs.

It does not need boots
to keep its feet warm and dry.

Does a musk ox wear an overcoat?

A musk ox doesn't need an overcoat because it has thick fur everywhere—even on its face.

It stays warm even when the weather is very cold.

Does a duck wear diapers?

No, silly!
Diapers are for babies.

Grown-ups put diapers on babies so they
don't pee and poop all over the place.

After a while, babies grow up and learn
to pee and poop in the bathroom.

Then there are no more diapers!

Only people wear clothing—
lots of different kinds.

They wear hats to protect their heads
from falling objects, from sun, and from cold.

They wear all kinds of coats to protect
their bodies from cold, wind, rain, and fire.

Animals do not need protection for their hands and feet, but people do. On their hands, they wear:

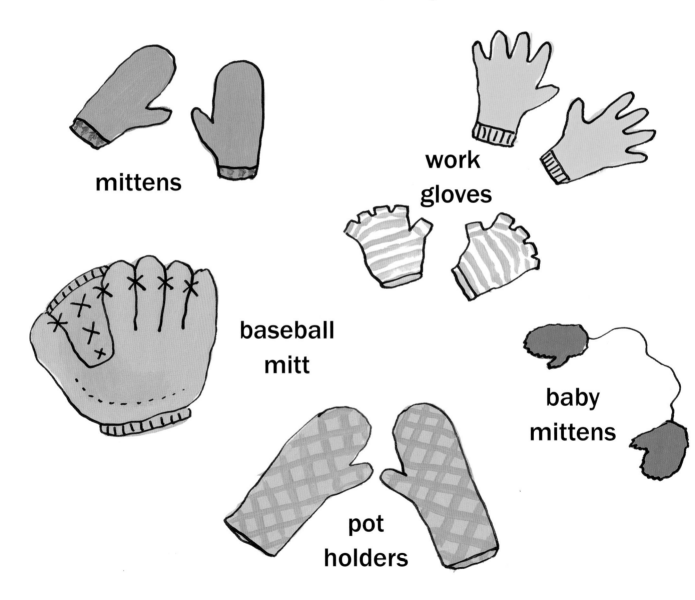

mittens

work gloves

baseball mitt

baby mittens

pot holders

On their feet, they wear:

work boots

slippers

flip-flops

rain boots

party shoes

baby booties

Some people put clothes
on their pets.

This dog is wearing a coat and a hat
to keep it warm.

But a wild dog, or a wild horse,
would never wear clothes.

People wear all different kinds of clothing—for work, for play, and for special occasions.

soccer player

waiter

carpenter

swimmer

diver

baseball player

underground worker

ballerina

doctor

chef

Sometimes people dress up in costumes.
Then they can pretend to be someone else.

Sometimes they dress up
for special occasions.

They wear party hats, party shoes,
party dresses, and suits.
So fancy!

What clothing do you like to wear?

Think 💡 About what everyone wears

This book compares people, who wear many different kinds of clothing, and animals, who don't wear clothes unless people dress them.

Compare and Contrast

When it is cold, people wear things to keep themselves warm.

- What do you wear to keep warm?
- What does a musk ox have to keep itself warm?
- What does a polar bear have to keep its feet warm?

Compare a dog and a wolf.

- Why does the dog wear a collar around its neck?
- Why doesn't a wolf wear a collar? Or a coat?

Compare a horse in the wild and a horse owned by people.

- What does the farm horse "wear" that the wild horse does not?
  Make a list. (Don't forget the shoes!)

Research

Go to a library or online and find out:

- how wool is made into cloth (look online under "turning wool into cloth")

People wear protective clothing when they work.

- Make a list of things that people wear to stay safe on the job.
  Ask some grown-ups you know for help.

Observe

Firefighters wear many things to protect themselves.

- Visit a firehouse, or find a book on firefighters.
  What protective clothing do you see?

What's the weather outside? What's everyone wearing?

- Think about what clothing you will need to be comfortable outdoors.
  Get dressed, and go out to play!

In a classroom, look at clothes the other kids wear.

- What colors do you see?

- What color is worn the most?

Write, Tell, or Draw

Think about dressing up.

- Describe and draw a costume you would like to wear.
  How will you act and feel in your costume?

Think about what you might like to do some day.

- Describe the things you would do and what special clothing you would need.